GW01071924

Dog-i
Object Lessons

Volume 2

Guide to 36 practical object lessons

Ideal for all age services, junior school and school assemblies

Written by Ian Jones

One Way UK

www.onewayuk.com

Ice House Christian Centre, Victor Street, Grimsby, DN32 7QN England
Tel: 01472 241068 / 01472 362810   Email: info@onewayuk.com   Website: www.onewayuk.com

Dog-in-a-Bag Object Lessons
Volume 2

A One Way UK Publication
First Published in Great Britain 2012

One Way UK Creative Ministries
Ice House Christian Centre
Victor Street
Grimsby
DN32 7QN

Sales Department: 01472 362810
Training Department: 01472 241068
Email: info@onewayuk.com
Website: www.onewayuk.com

Written by Ian Jones

Cover artwork by Peter Gray

Copyright ©2012 One Way UK Ltd

ISBN 978-904172-10-9

Introduction
Using the Dog-in-a-Bag Puppet

Since I started using puppets, one of my favourite and most versatile of them all is the Dog-in-a-Bag puppet. This adorable character is very easy to use and with a little preparation and practice can be your friend for life and a companion in ministry wherever you go. Whether you are in a church, school or residential home, the Dog-in-a-Bag puppet is sure to grab and hold everyone's attention whilst you share with them a Bible story or gospel message.

I use the whispering technique, with the puppet whispering to me and then I repeat what they have said. To be effective, a believable relationship must exist between you, the puppet and with your audience. This is best achieved by just spending time with the puppet on your hand, chatting with it and if possible working in front of a mirror. This gives you instant feedback and helps you to find out how different movements of your hand can create different mannerisms and emotions.

It is a partnership, your body language is essential as you listen to and tell the story together. Always keep the puppet involved. Even when you are talking make sure that the puppet is engaged, listening and reacting to what you say.

Placing an object in the bag enables you to teach a lesson using the object which will be more memorable and fun. Also, the next time you use them, the audience will be wanting to know what is in the bag as soon as they appear. This book includes a full script and 36 individual lessons with the teaching point, object and Bible passage.

Have fun and God bless you in your ministry

Ian Jones

INDEX

Complete starter script – Freedom (string)

No. Subject	Object	Bible Verse	In Prop Kit
1 Celebration	Party Popper	Luke 15:11-31	Yes
2 Crucifixion	Nail	Luke 23:33	Yes
3 David and Goliath	Stone	1 Samuel 17:40	Yes
4 Enjoying God's Goodness	Sweet	Isaiah 40:5	
5 Eternal Life	Key	Matthew 16:19	Yes
6 Facing Fears	Balloon	2 Corinthians 7:5-6	Yes
7 Faith and Deeds	Business Card	James 2:18b	Yes
8 Feeding the 5000	Toy/Plastic Fish	Matthew 14:13-21	
9 Forgiveness	Soap	Acts 22:16	Yes
10 Forgiveness (2)	Rubber/Eraser	1 John 1:9	Yes
11 Forgiving Others	Pen	Matthew 18:21-22	
12 God's Wisdom	Jigsaw Piece	1 Corinthians 2:10	Yes
13 God's Family	Family Photo	Ephesians 2:19	Yes
14 God's Help	Plaster	Luke 1:37	Yes
15 God's Invitation	Party Invitation	Luke 14:8	Yes
16 God's Plan for Us	Pocket Diary	Jeremiah 29:11-13	Yes
17 God's Purpose for Us	Paper Clip	Colossians 1:16-17	Yes
18 Greatest Commandment	Clothes Peg	Matthew 22:36-40	Yes

No. Subject	Object	Bible Verse	In Prop Kit
19 Guilt and Shame	Sun Glasses	Psalm 38:4	
20 I'm Special	Badge	John 3:16	Yes
21 Jesus Light of the World	Wind Up Torch	John 8:12	
22 Judging Others	Wrapping Paper	Matthew 7:1	Yes
23 Parable of Lost Coin	Coin	Luke 15:8-10	Yes
24 New Life	Egg	John 3:3	Yes
25 Obedience	Small Mirror	James 1:23-24	
26 Prayer	Mobile Phone	Ephesians 6:18	
27 Price Jesus Paid	Chocolate Drops	Hebrews 9:28	
28 Putting God First	Ball	Matthew 22:37	Yes
29 Reaping What You Sow	Packet of Seeds	Galatians 6:7	Yes
30 Worry	Watch	Matthew 6:25	
31 Resurrection	Nothing!	Matthew 28:6	Yes!
32 Rich Fool	Bone	Luke 12:18	
33 Running the Race	Medal	Hebrews 12:1	Yes
34 Salvation	Passport	Acts 4:12	
35 Taste and See	Biscuit	Psalm 34:8	
36 Way to Heaven	Compass	Psalm 143:8	

Rover – Freedom

Object: Piece of string
Bible Verse: Galatians 5:1

Hello Rover, are you going to come out of your bag today and say hello to everyone? **(Rover shakes head "no" in bag)**
No, why not? **(Rover whispers from inside bag)**
You are a bit busy today **(Rover nods)**
Surely you have got time to come out and say hello, everyone has come here to see you!
(Rover peeps out with a small piece of string visible around his nose)
That's better. Wait a minute, what is that round your nose? **(lower bag a bit more to reveal more of Rover and even more string around him!)**
Rover, what have you been up to? **(Rover whispers)**
You're a bit tied up at the moment **(Rover nods)**
I can see that, but what are you doing with all that string? **(Rover whispers)**
Your bag was beginning to feel a bit lived in **(Rover nods then whispers again)**
So you decided to have a bit of a sort out **(Rover nods)**
You mean you have finally decided to get rid of some of that junk that you keep in there **(Rover stares at you with mouth wide open)**
I'm sorry **(Rover whispers)**
It's not junk **(Rover shakes his head and whispers)**
It's just that you haven't found a use for it all yet! **(Rover nods)**
I see, but if you don't mind me asking, how is it going?
(Rover looks a bit down, then whispers)
It's harder than you thought it would be! **(Rover nods)**
Well, it has been quite a long time since you had a clean out, and you do seem to have collected rather a lot of junk **(Rover glares at you)**
I mean stuff **(Rover nods)**
And what are you going to do with it all, once you have sorted it all out?
(Rover whispers)
You are going to put it all in my house **(Rover nods)**
I thought that might have been your plan and you can forget it
(Rover looks shocked and then tries to snuggle up to you)
And don't try that, if you think you can get round me that easily! **(Rover nods)**
Erm… we will see…
And anyway, you haven't explained why you are all tied up with string?
(Rover whispers)
It was when you started to tidy up and sort things out **(Rover nods and whispers)**
That's when it started to go wrong, oh dear! **(Rover nods and whispers)**
The string just wouldn't behave **(Rover whispers)**
And the more you tried **(Rover whisper)**
The more you got into a bigger and bigger mess! **(Rover cries on your shoulder)**

Now there there, I am sure we can sort you out
(Rover looks up and tries to lick you)
Get off, get off!
The problem is, that the more we try and sort out our messes, the worse they seem to get! **(Rover nods and whispers)**
What? So you think it would be better all-round if you didn't do anything at all! **(Rover nods)**
No, that's not what I meant. What I meant was that, we do need to sort out the messes we make, but not in our own strength **(Rover whispers)**
No, you don't get some other mug to do it for you!
We ask God to be our helper **(Rovers jaw drops and whispers)**
Yes, He would do that for us all. Wow.
You see, God doesn't want us to get all tied up in the mess that we make of things. In the book of Galatians, Paul tells us about the people there and how they were getting themselves all tied up in the old religious rules, like you have been with all that string. Galatians, chapter 5:1 says "It is for freedom that Christ has set us free" **(Rover whispers)**
Yes, when we ask God to be involved in our lives and say sorry to Him for all of the bad things we have done, God promises to hear our prayers and forgive us.
Then we can be free of guilt and shame **(Rover whispers)**
Yes, just like you, once you have escaped from that string **(Rover whispers)**
Yes that is really good news isn't it! **(Rover Nods, then whispers)**
You are going back to your tidying up now **(Rover whispers)**
But you are going to pray and ask God to help you do it **(Rover nods)**
Well done, I am sure that He will **(Rover disappears back into his bag)**

You know, if your life feels a bit like Rover's sometimes, in a mess and all tied up, then why don't you ask God to help you too?

1. Celebration
   Object: Party Popper   **Prop Kit - Yes**
   Bible Verse: Luke 15:11-31

Question to Doggie – "Why have you got a party popper in your bag?"

Doggie's answer – He is going to a big party, a great celebration!

Your answer – Who's party is it, why the celebration? Let Doggie help tell the story of the lost son and that there will be a similar party when we make the decision to turn back to God rather than doing what we want and let Jesus into our lives. In Heaven there won't be party poppers but there will be a multitude of angels singing and praising God to welcome us home.

2. Crucifixion
   Object: Nail   **Prop Kit - Yes**
   Bible Verse: Luke 23:33

Question to Doggie – "Why have you got a nail in your bag today?"

Doggie's answer – He was going to do some DIY, but it was very difficult with paws and the harder he tried the bigger the mess he made.

Your answer – Share how that is often like our own lives. We try and do things by ourselves, and often we can do so much better and more when we ask others to help us. Tell how no matter how hard we try, we can never work our way to be good enough for God. That is why Jesus was nailed to a cross and died for us. He took our sins on Himself so that we can be accepted by God.

3. David and Goliath
Object: Stone
Bible Verse: 1 Samuel 17:40

Prop Kit - Yes

Question to Doggie – "Why have you got a stone in your bag?"

Doggie's answer – It reminds you of your favourite story in the Bible. When David was the underdog and won a great victory for His people.

Your answer – Summarise the story of David and Goliath with Doggie reminding you of all the important parts. Say there are often Goliaths around even today (Doggie can look scared and hide). They may be bullies, or problems, or fears, but we have to face up to them and God promises to help us with His Holy Spirit.

4. Enjoying God's Goodness
Object: Sweet
Bible Verse: Isaiah 40:5

Question to Doggie – "Why have you got a sweet in your bag?"

Doggie's answer – It is his favourite sweet, which he has had since his last birthday/Easter/Christmas (whichever is a while ago). He loves to look at it and think about the lovely thing inside.

Your answer – Understand that it is nice to have special things, and lovely to look at them. But, have you thought about opening it? Explain that some people treat the Bible in the same way. They have it but never open it and enjoy the wonderful things that are inside. Why not open it and let God show us His wonderful truths about Himself, Jesus and the plans He has for us!

5. Eternal Life
    Object: Key   **Prop Kit - Yes**
    Bible Verse: Matthew 16:19

Question to Doggie – "Why have you got a key in your bag?"

Doggie's answer – He has had to put a new lock on his kennel, the neighbourhood is getting a bit "ruff".

Your answer – Talk about how keys are used to lock things up, to keep them safe and to stop people from getting into our homes. Talk about how keys are also used to open doors, get into special places. The Bible talks about us having the "Keys to the Kingdom of Heaven". Have we locked the door of our heart or opened it to let Jesus in?

6. Facing Fears
    Object: Balloon   **Prop Kit - Yes**
    Bible Verse: 2 Corinthians 7:5-6

Question to Doggie – "Why have you got a balloon in your bag?"

Doggie's answer – He has always been frightened of balloons, but he thought it would help him face his fears if he got used to having one in his bag.

Your answer – Explain that we can often be frightened of things and that is nothing to be ashamed of. This passage from the Bible reminds us that when there is fighting around us and inside we feel very frightened, we need to trust God and he promises to comfort us.

7. Faith and Deeds
   Object: Business Card   **Prop Kit - Yes**
   Bible Verse: James 2:18b

Question to Doggie – "What is this in your bag? Why have you got a business card?"

Doggie's answer – Sometimes it is so hard to be good. He thought it would help people to know he was a Christian!

Your answer – We become a Christian when we know we have done wrong and say sorry to Jesus, ask him to be our special friend and put Him first in our lives. We put our trust and faith in Him. This faith is shown by how we live. We can't just tell people by having a card or wearing a cross. It's how we live. Hard? Yes, but with God's help – the Holy Spirit, we can do it!

8. Feeding the 5000
   Object: Toy/Plastic Fish
   Bible Verse: Matthew 14:13-21

Question to Doggie – "What is that smell coming from your bag this morning? Oh no, why have you got a fish in your bag?"

Doggie's answer – It is his lunch! The butchers shop was closed and this was all you could find as he was really hungry!

Your answer – Share the story with him about the time when there were a lot of very hungry people with Jesus. About 5,000 men, plus women and children, and how He fed them with just five loaves and two fishes. Wasn't it amazing how Jesus could feed them all. When we trust Him with everything from our basic needs to our biggest problems, He can work miracles, we just need to ask Him!

9. Forgiveness
   Object: Soap   **Prop Kit - Yes**
   Bible Verse: Acts 22:16

Question to Doggie – "Why have you got a bar of soap in your bag, why are you crying?"

Doggie's answer – He is very upset because of something bad he has done, and he read in the book of Acts that you can have your sins washed away and he thought the soap would help!

Your answer – Were you crying because you are really sorry (No, the soap got in his eyes!) Just as soap can make us clean by washing away the dirt on the outside of us, when we say sorry to God, He can make us clean on the inside by forgiving our sins.

10. Forgiveness (2)
   Object: Rubber/Eraser   **Prop Kit - Yes**
   Bible Verse: 1 John 1:9

Question to Doggie – "Why have you got a rubber in your bag, have you been doing your homework?"

Doggie's answer – No! He has got it in his bag to remind him what the Bible teaches about forgiveness. Like, when we make a mistake writing, we can use a rubber to rub the mistake out, when we do the wrong thing in our lives, we can say sorry and ask Jesus to forgive us.

Your answer – But, can't your writing get a bit messy with all the rubbing out that you're doing? Yes, but with Jesus everything is made perfect.

11. Forgiving Others
Object: Pen
Bible Verse: Matthew 18:21-22

Question to Doggie – "Why have you got a pen in your bag, have you been doing your homework?"

Doggie's answer – Ooops, he had forgotten all about that! No, he is feeling really sad as some of the other dogs have been very unkind to him. He has been using the pen to make a list and write down all the bad things to help him remember them.

Your answer – Doesn't that make you even sadder? The Bible reading today reminds us that we should forgive each other and not just seven times but seventy times seven times. Keep pen but this time to make a list of good things.

12. God's Wisdom
Object: Jigsaw Piece   Prop Kit - Yes
Bible Verse: 1 Corinthians 2:10

Question to Doggie – "Why have you got a piece from a jigsaw puzzle in your bag?"

Doggie's answer – He is not very happy. He has been trying to do the puzzle and he is missing some pieces and he hasn't even got the picture!

Your answer – Sometimes life can be a bit like this. We struggle to see God's big picture as we are only looking at one very small piece – our lives, today, here and now. But we need to pray that God will reveal to us everything by His Holy Spirit

13. God's Family
Object: Family Photo   Prop Kit - Yes
Bible Verse: Ephesians 2:19

Question to Doggie – "What have you got there? Go on show it to me!"

Doggie's answer – It is a family portrait! He loves his family and they are very special to him.

Your answer – Agree, families are very special. How can you tell a family? Answer – "They all have the same fleas!" Yes, you might have, but a better answer is that you all have the same characteristics and you love and care for each other. Today's verse reminds us that in a family we are not strangers, we all are special and we belong there. Just as we do in God's family.

14. God's Help
Object: Plaster   Prop Kit – Yes
Bible Verse: Luke 1:37

Question to Doggie – "Why have you got a plaster in your bag, have you been hurt?"

Doggie's answer – No, he is fine… nothing really the matter… nothing that he can't fix himself with a plaster.

Your answer – Really? Is he sure? It is just that for nothing he is looking very sad, and whining a lot. Don't you think that just maybe, you might need someone to help you? Expand on how we need to invite God to be involved in all we do and that rather try and patch things up ourselves, ask God to help for nothing is impossible with God.

15. God's Invitation
Object: Party Invitation   Prop Kit - Yes
Bible Verse: Luke 14:8

Question to Doggie – "Oh Doggie, have you been invited to a party, how exciting!"

Doggie's answer – He is very excited and can't wait to get there. He must be early so that he can be one of the top dogs and get to sit at the best place nearest all the food and his birthday buddy!

Your answer – Explain the reading today is about humility, doggie can say he knows all about humidity, you try living in this bag wearing a fur coat in the middle of summer! No, humility. Talk through the story involving and interacting with doggie and ending with him agreeing to try it at the party.

16. God's Plan for us
Object: Pocket Diary   Prop Kit - Yes
Bible Verse: Jeremiah 29:11-13

Question to Doggie – "Why have you got a diary in your bag?"

Doggie's answer – He has a very busy social life and he needs it to put all his plans in.

Your answer – But there is hardly anything in it! He likes to keep it like that so that he is free if anything turns up. Suggest he uses it to record where he buries all his bones. Doggie says no, because if Scamp from across the road got it he would know where he had hidden all his bones. Yes, but so would he, good point! Whilst we can make plans, we should trust God as He knows all His plans for us and these are to prosper and help us, not to harm us.

17. God's Purpose for Us
Object: Large Paper Clip
Bible Verse: Colossians 1:16-17

Prop Kit - Yes

Question to Doggie – "What have you got this large paperclip in your bag for?

Doggie's answer – To remind him of the verse from Colossians "that He holds all creation together", hence the paper clip!

Your answer – Exclaim, that you sort of see his point, you think that God is probably using more than a paper clip to hold the universe together – even a very large paperclip! But he is right really. This paperclip is just an ordinary piece of wire that has been taken and shaped to make something for a special purpose, just like we have.

18. Greatest Commandment
Object: Clothes Peg
Bible Verse: Matthew 22:36-40

Prop Kit - Yes

Question to Doggie – "Why on earth have you got a clothes peg in your bag? I know it can get a bit whiffy in there but…!

Doggie's answer – Very funny, very funny. But no, it is to remind everyone of a very important passage from the Bible.

Your answer – Let him explain the passage on the Greatest Commandment. At the end sum up by saying "Yes, I agree that they are the two Greatest Commandments, but I still don't understand why you have a peg to remind you of them?" His reply is that on them HANG all the law and the prophets!

19. Guilt and Shame
Object: Sun Glasses
Bible Verse: Psalm 38:4

Question to Doggie – "Hey Mr Cool, what's with the shades today?"

Doggie's answer – He has decided to change his image… and the sun/light is very bright… any other excuse as to why he would be wearing sun glasses.

Your answer – Play along, but in the end ask him what the real reason is why he is wearing the glasses. Let him explain that he has done something wrong and he is ashamed of it. What can we do? Live weighed down with the guilt or confess what we have done and say sorry and ask for forgiveness? It may be hard, particularly if the problem is that you have bitten the postman and he might not be too keen on you getting close to him again!

20. I'm Special
Object: Badge   **Prop Kit - Yes**
Bible Verse: John 3:16

Question to Doggie – "What have you got in your bag today? WOW a badge! What does it say on it, *I'm Special*"

Doggie's answer – He asks you to guess where he got it from.

Your answer – Have you been to "Crufts" and you received it there! No, well where from then? From church! You learnt a very special verse in the Bible that tells us that we are very special, that God sent His only Son because he loves us so much. Wow if He did that for us, we must be very special to Him.

21. Jesus Light of the World
Object: Wind Up Torch
Bible Verse: John 8:12

Question to Doggie – "What have you got in your bag today?"

Doggie's answer – It is very dark in the bag and you know how frightened I get in the dark, so he thought it was a good idea to torch, but it doesn't work!

Your answer – Have a look at it and explain that it is a wind up torch. Ask him if he has tried winding it up? Ah, no. Ask helper to wind it up and show Doggie that it does work now. Say how it can be frightening in the dark and how easy it is to trip up and stumble when you can't see where you are going. But it can only be light or dark, when there is light, there is no darkness. In light, you can see your way clearly and not get lost or fall. Need to stay in light. A wind up torch needs you to keep recharging it. We need to keep close to Jesus and be powered by Him.

22. Judging Others
Object: Wrapping Paper   **Prop Kit - Yes**
Bible Verse: Matthew 7:1

Question to Doggie – "Why have you got that old piece of wrapping paper in your bag?"

Doggie's answer – He explains how he has kept it to remind him of the present he got for Christmas/his birthday that didn't look very nice. He didn't think he would like it because he was judging it by how it looked.

Your answer – Explain that we can easily judge things by how they look on the outside both presents and people. We should open the present to find out what is inside and get to know people rather than judging them on their appearance. We will be judged as we judge others.

23. Parable of Lost Coin
Object: Coin
Prop Kit - Yes
Bible Verse: Luke 15:8-10

Question to Doggie – "Why are you looking so sad?"

Doggie's answer – He has lost his favourite coin!

Your answer – Oh dear, have you really looked everywhere? Reminds me of a story Jesus told. Tell the parable of the lost coin with Doggie asking questions like "what did she do..." etc. Emphasise the joy when one sinner repents. Put coin back in bag, not to spend but to remind him of the story.

24. New Life
Object: Egg
Prop Kit - Yes
Bible Verse: John 3:3

Question to Doggie – "Why have you got an egg in your bag?"

Doggie's answer – That it reminds him of new life.

Your answer – Read the passage and share how, whilst it is good to learn more about God, the most important thing is that we have a personal relationship with Him. We have to move on from what we know in our heads to what we believe in our hearts. It is only by being born again that we can ever see the kingdom of God.

25. Obedience
   ### Object: Small mirror
   ### Bible Verse: James 1:23-24

Question to Doggie – "Say how smart he is looking and why the sudden interest in his appearance with the mirror in his bag, is it a girlfriend?

Doggie's answer – No! He explains that he was reading from the book of James, and it says "that you should look in a mirror and improve your appearance"

Your answer – Ask him if he is really sure that is what it says. Read the passage making the point that what James is really saying is that listening to God and then not obeying Him, is like looking at yourself in the mirror then not doing anything to improve your appearance. We must listen AND obey! Hard? Yes but with God's help we can do it.

26. Prayer
   ### Object: Mobile Phone
   ### Bible Verse: Ephesians 6:18

Question to Doggie – "What's this in your bag a new mobile phone?"

Doggie's answer – Yes, it is a new Blueberry (or think of another name). He bought it off Lassie, it does everything! List off all new functions, apps etc., and Lassie said I can even talk to God with it!

Your answer – Really, are you sure? It's just that in the Bible, in the book, Ephesians, it says "that we should pray at all times in the Spirit" and doesn't say anything about needing the latest mobile phone to do it. We can pray anywhere at any time to God. I think Lassie has sold you a dud! Doggie takes phone back and drops it in his bag, ask what are you going to do with it, he is going to take it back to Lassie and get the bones back that he gave him for it!

27. Price Jesus Paid
Object: Chocolate Drops
Bible Verse: Hebrews 9:28

Question to Doggie – "What is the matter with you, why are you so quiet?

Outline of story – He explains that he was very hungry, so he went to the shop (name local large supermarket). Then he got chased, on the way home? No, out of the shop! Ask why, the sweet he got was on offer, Buy one get one free, and he picked up one of the free ones! That's why he was chased. But it was ok. How? He gave the security guard your name! Explain that that was stealing, and how you will pay the guard for the sweet. Finish by saying that when Jesus died on the cross, it was for all the bad things we do, like stealing. We need to say sorry and ask God to forgive us, and not do it again.

28. Putting God First
Object: Ball   **Prop Kit – Yes**
Bible Verse: Matthew 22:37

Question to Doggie – "Why have you got a ball in your bag, are you going to play in the park?

Doggie's answer – It's my favourite ball, go everywhere together. Most important thing to him.

Your answer – Explain how it is very easy to have things that become very important to us. But in Matthew, Jesus said the most important commandment is to love God with all your heart, soul and mind. We need to put God first and not let other things take God's place.

29. Reaping What You Sow
   Object: Packet of Seeds   **Prop Kit - Yes**
   Bible Verse: Galatians 6:7

Question to Doggie – "What have you got in your bag today?"

Doggie's answer – He has been reading the part in the bible about reaping what you sow. Scamp has sold him some bone seeds so that he can grow his own bones and then he will be reaping what he sows!"

Your answer – Ah, did he! I don't think that Paul's letter to the Galatians was about growing plants, or bones! When he talked about reaping what you sow, he meant that if all that you do is just to please yourself, then you will not reap any blessings from God. You cannot fool God! God sees everything we do and why we do it. So, if we sow and do good things for God then you will reap blessings from Him.

30. Worry
   Object: Watch
   Bible Verse: Matthew 6:25

Question to Doggie – "Hey, is that a new watch you have got!"

Doggie's answer – Oh yes, he is so busy and has so many things to remember that he worries a lot and needs to keep his eye on the watch all the time.

Your answer – Recall passage and point out that we are special to God and that He knows us and will provide for us. He does so for the birds and we are more valuable than they are. We must trust Him for everything and not worry.

31. Resurrection
Object: Nothing   **Prop Kit – Yes!**
Bible Verse: Matthew 28:6

Question to Doggie – "What have you got in your bag today?"

Doggie's answer – Search bag and find nothing! Act really surprised.

Your answer – Let Doggie explain to you that that is how Mary felt when she went back to the tomb and found it empty too. When Jesus died and was buried, people thought that that was the end of Him. But wrong, Jesus rose again from the dead, He is alive!

32. Rich Fool
Object: Bone
Bible Verse: Luke 12:18

Question to Doggie – "Why have you got a bone in your bag?"

Doggie's answer – He has a large collection of bones now and when he saw this one he just couldn't resist it. He is going to have to dig an even bigger hole now to store them all in!

Your answer – What about today's reading? Jesus told a story about a rich farmer that kept on storing more and more, building bigger and bigger barns. He used it as a warning to us that it is a fool who spends all their time building up money and things on earth but does not have a rich relationship with God.
So, what is more important, a rich relationship with God or lots of bones?

33. Running the Race
Object: Medal
Bible Verse: Hebrews 12:1

Prop Kit - Yes

Question to Doggie – "There is a gold medal here in your bag, is it yours?"

Doggie's answer – Yes, he was given it when he completed his Kennel Club obedience course! It was very hard and he had to keep going every week till he had finished it.

Your answer – That is like following God's plan for our life. We must run with perseverance, just as the verse in Hebrews 12:1 it is only by keeping our eyes fixed on Jesus that we can complete what God has got planned for us. His reward isn't a gold medal, it is the promise of eternal life with Him!

34. Salvation
Object: Passport
Bible Verse: Acts 4:12

Question to Doggie – "Hey, why have you got your passport with you in your bag today, are you going on holiday?"

Doggie's answer – Yes, he is going to visit his friend a Border Collie, hence why he needs his passport to go across the border!

Your answer – Explain that he might not need his passport to visit his friend, but you do need a passport to get into other foreign countries. The Bible verse reminds us that Jesus is the only way to Heaven and we need Jesus, like we need a passport, to get there.

35. Taste and See
Object: Biscuit
Bible Verse: Psalm 34:8

Question to Doggie – "Why have you got a half-eaten biscuit in your bag?"

Doggie's answer – You were just in the middle of your snack!

Your answer – Biscuits look lovely and are so nice but the best part is tasting and eating them! Remind me of Psalm 34:8 Taste and See that the Lord is good. Oh, the joys of those who trust in Him. So, don't just look at the Bible, don't just think about nibbling around the edges, take a great big bite and Taste and See that the Lord IS GOOD!

36. Way to Heaven
Object: Compass
Bible Verse: Psalm 143:8

Question to Doggie – "Why have you got a compass in your bag?"

Doggie's answer – He is fed up of going round and round in circles and getting lost, so he has got a compass to help him find the right way.

Your answer – It is very easy to get lost and to end up going the wrong way. As a compass tells us which path we should take, the Bible can guide and lead us to make the right decisions and choices as to what we should do. In life, there are many things that can distract us or lead us away from God and His way, but we need to listen to Him and obey his commands and He promises to always be with us and to never leave us.

Notes

Notes

Notes